WOMEN IN THE ARMED FORCES

WORLD WAR II HISTORY BOOK 4TH GRADE CHILDREN'S HISTORY

In war movies, we usually see mostly men making decisions and doing the fighting. But in World War II many women took important roles, too. Read on and learn about women soldiers around the world in the Second World War.

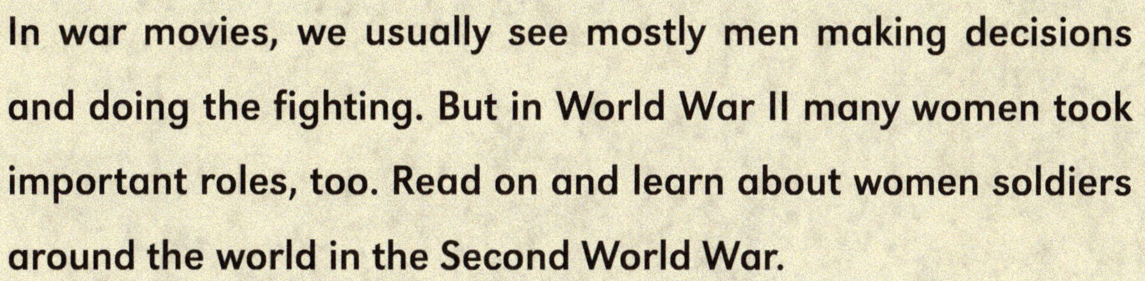

THE DEMANDS OF WAR

When World War II started, in 1939, most of the world was still very conservative about what women could and should do. Men were supposed work at jobs to earn money while women stayed home to take care of the children, or maybe worked as nurses or teachers.

All that changed with the total engagement of World War II. The countries that fought each other had to use every resource they could find. As more and more men went into the military, women got to take their jobs in factories, on farms, and in offices.

As the war went on, women in many countries joined the military themselves, sometimes even in combat roles. By the end of the war, hundreds of thousands of women had put on their countries' uniforms, besides the millions who took on war work in factories and growing food for the troops.

GA
CTOR
RCFT

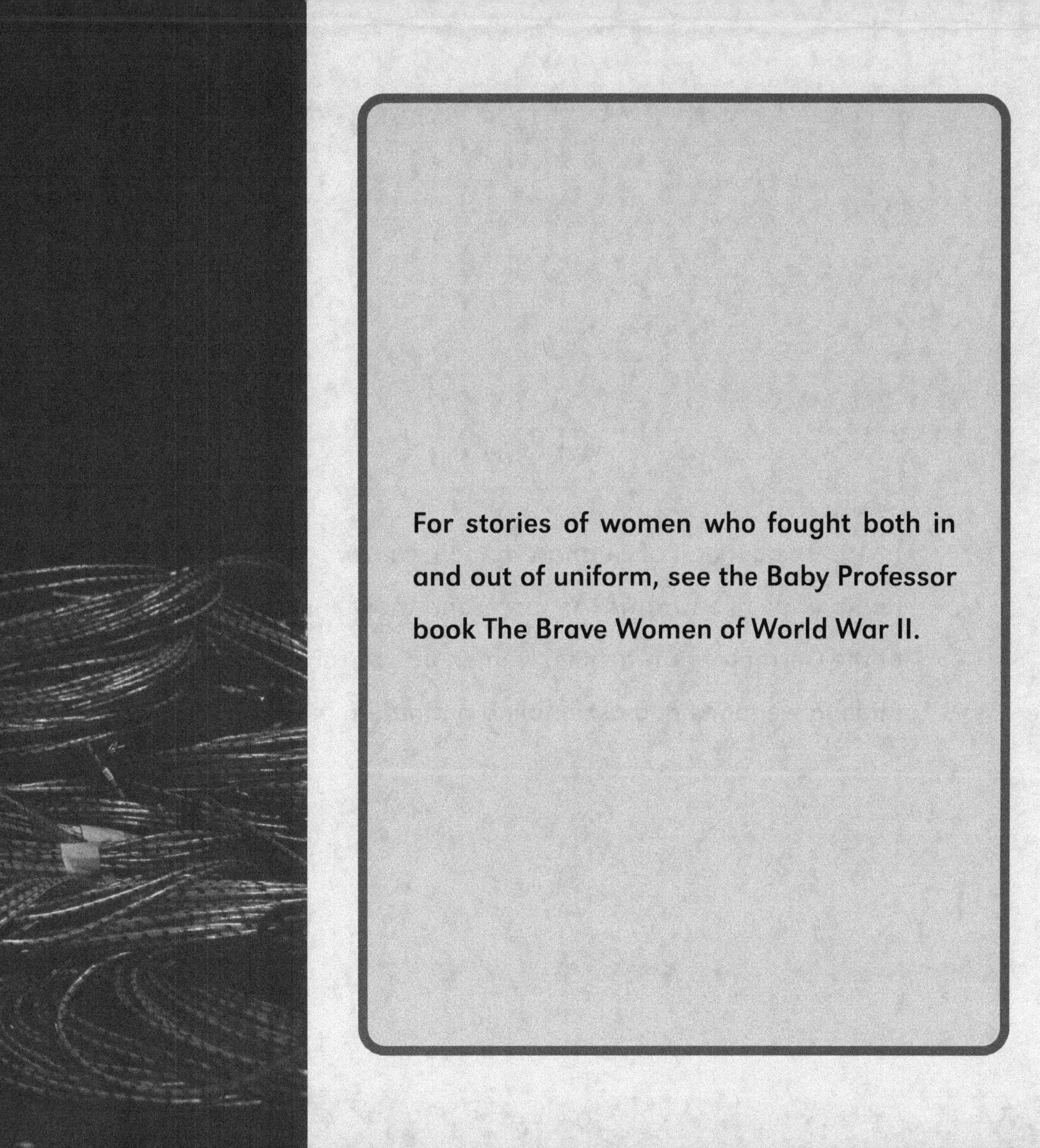

For stories of women who fought both in and out of uniform, see the Baby Professor book The Brave Women of World War II.

GERMANY

In 1939 about half of German women were working outside the home, mainly on farms. As more and more men became part of the German war machine, women had to take over their jobs making weapons and assembling ammunition.

MILITARY PRODUCTION DURING WORLD WAR II

Germany had many military units for women, including combat units. More than 500,000 women were in uniform in the German army. About the same number worked in air defense, operating spotlights, reporting on approaching planes, and doing similar tasks, but not usually firing the guns. Almost as many women worked as nurses in military hospitals. Hundreds served as guards in prisoner-of-war camps and in the horrible camps where the Germans executed millions of "undesirable" people, especially Jews, homosexuals, and people of certain cultural groups.

UNITED KINGDOM

Many British women joined the military in World War II. As well as women working in factories and in other jobs to replace men who had gone to fight, there were almost half a million women in uniform.

FORDSON TRACTOR WITH MEMBERS OF BRITISH WOMEN'S LAND ARMY
BBD 260
Fordson

A.T.S.
W.L.A.
Clothing Coupons   160
"   Allowance £12·10·0
Gratuity   8/6 per month
Keeps all Uniform bar
Greatcoat, Skirt, Tunic
1 week's paid leave
20-35
None!
None!
Keeps only 1 Shirt, 1 pair
shoes, 1 Greatcoat
None

WOMEN'S LAND ARMY IN BRITAIN

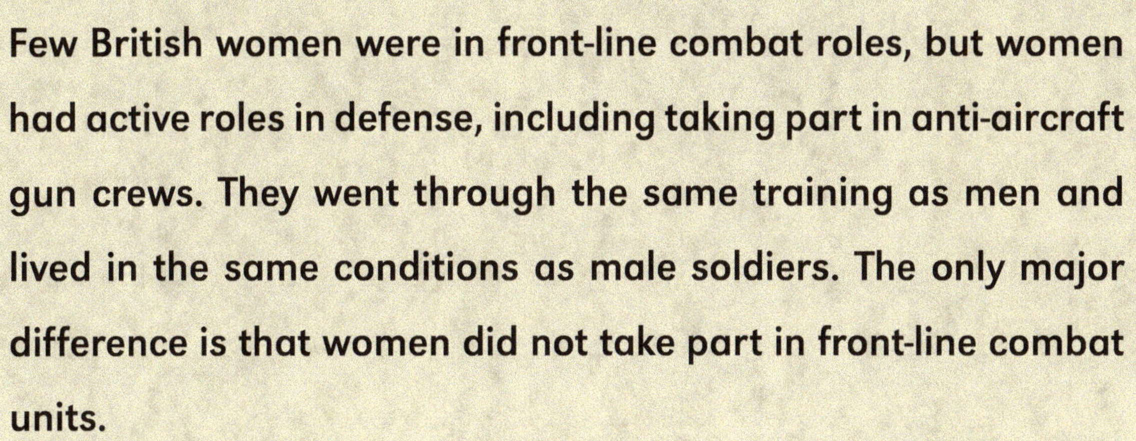

Few British women were in front-line combat roles, but women had active roles in defense, including taking part in anti-aircraft gun crews. They went through the same training as men and lived in the same conditions as male soldiers. The only major difference is that women did not take part in front-line combat units.

Two areas stand out where British women made important contributions:

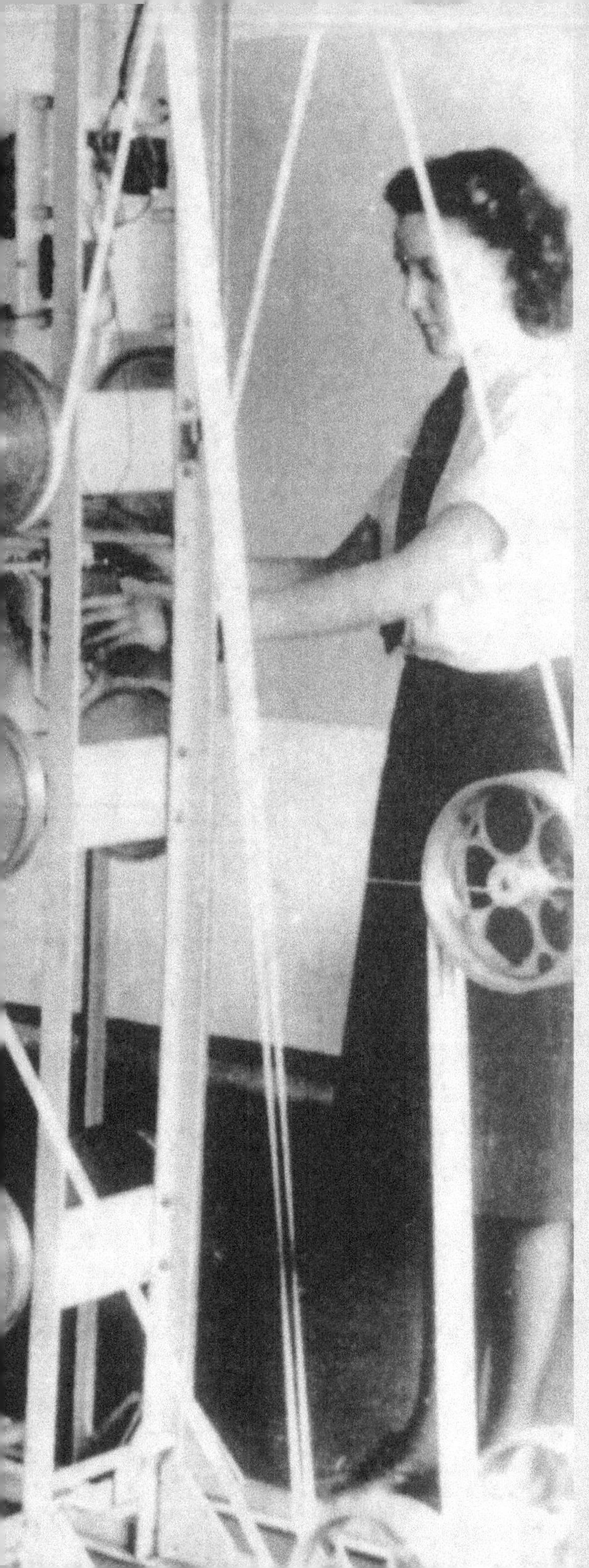

At Bletchley, as part of a secret program, a group of women code-breakers helped to crack the code system the German military was using to send messages to and from its units. Knowing the commands sent to enemy units let the Allied forces take appropriate steps to respond.

Women proved especially good at interpreting aerial photographs. Spy planes took the photos of German cities and military positions, and then a team had to try to figure out what was in the images. Women worked as equals of men in this project, and made important discoveries about hidden German positions, weak points in German defenses, and secret stockpiles of bombs that the Allies could then attack and destroy.

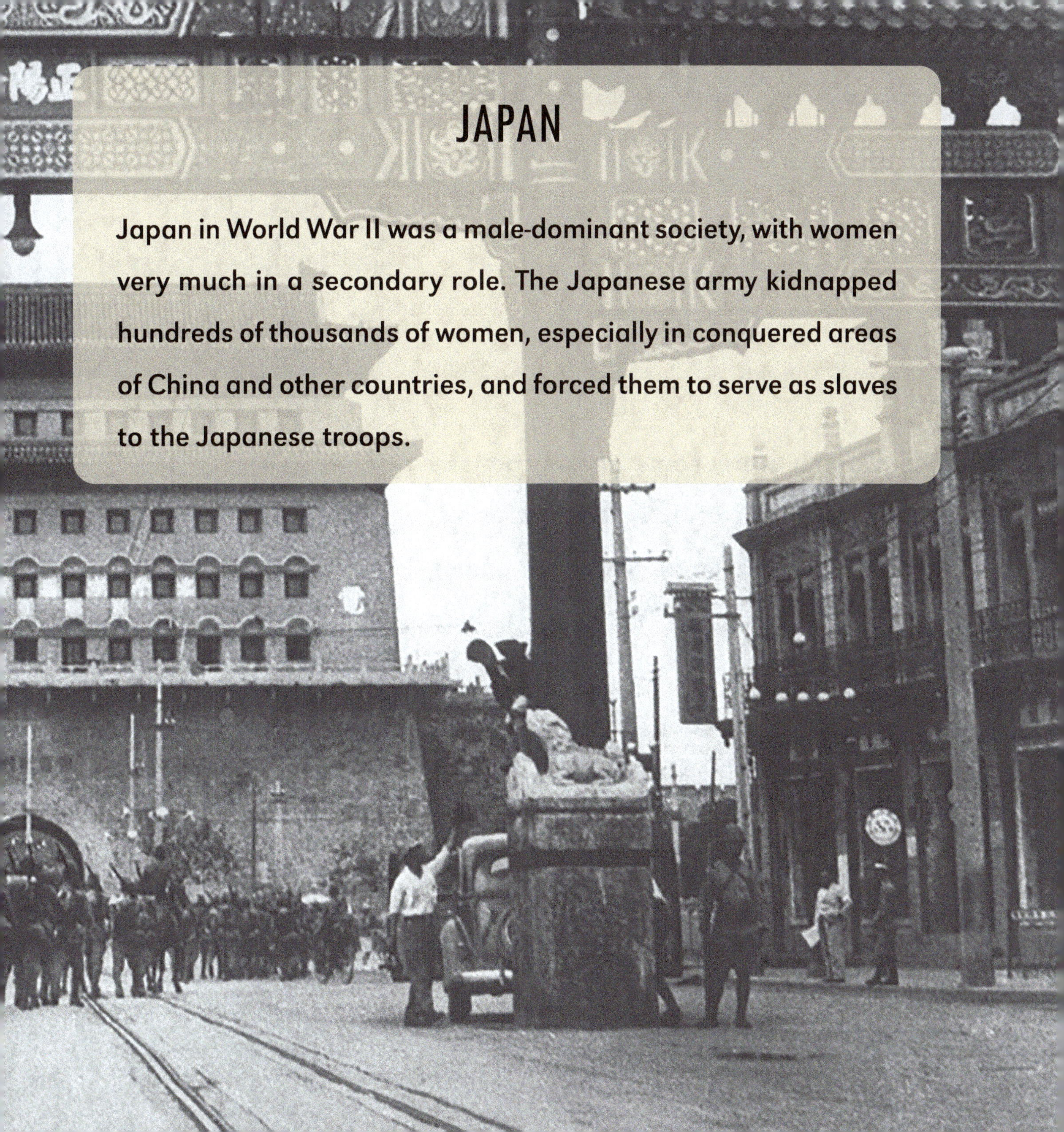

JAPAN

Japan in World War II was a male-dominant society, with women very much in a secondary role. The Japanese army kidnapped hundreds of thousands of women, especially in conquered areas of China and other countries, and forced them to serve as slaves to the Japanese troops.

The women were sometimes promised good jobs in factories or as waitresses, and then were taken far from their homes and forced to do whatever the soldiers wanted.

UNITED STATES

The United States entered World War II in 1941. Between then and 1945, about 350,000 women served in the United States military.

Most of the women in uniform still did traditionally "female" jobs. They worked as typists and clerks, delivered the mail, and answered phones, and served as nurses in hospitals that were sometimes close to the front lines. There were no women combat units.

SOVIET UNION

The Soviet Union started bringing women into its military units early in World War II. Almost one million Soviet women served in uniform, mostly as nurses and medics. However, over 300,000 were members of anti-aircraft units. They performed all duties, including firing the guns.

Some Soviet women flew bomber planes and drove tanks and other combat vehicles. Female snipers became famous as deadly shots.

OTHER COUNTRIES

AUSTRALIA

The country formed hundreds of women's units during World War II. Australian women did everything the men did in their country's armed forces, except go into combat.

CANADA

The Canadian Women's Army Corps was created in 1941. It included women who served as nurses, drivers, cooks, office workers, telephonists, and in other support roles. By 1942, women were able to join the Navy and Air Force. Over 50,000 Canadian women served during the war.

CANADIAN WOMEN'S ARMY CORPS

C. H. PETCH

Women had to meet requirements that included:

⇒ Be older than 18 and younger than 41

⇒ Be of good health

⇒ Be at least five feet tall and of "appropriate" weight

⇒ Have at least an education equal to first year of high school

⇒ Be of good character and have no criminal record

FINLAND

Women in the Finnish military mainly served in defensive roles, as nurses, air raid wardens, cooks, and in other support duties. Lotta Svärd, their organization, was the largest voluntary women's group involved in the war. Its members did everything to support the fighting forces, but did not themselves fire weapons.

LOTTA SVÄRD STATUE

ITALY

Many women in Italy joined in resistance movements that fought against the fascist Italian government of Benito Mussolini, which was on the side of Germany. Of the 200,000 members of the Resistance, at least 35,000 were women. Most of the women performed support work, and none were allowed high leadership positions. However, some women were part of small fighting groups that would attack enemy troops or try to destroy bridges or other essential equipment. Over 650 women died in combat or were executed after they were captured.

The fascist government of Mussolini mainly honored women as "baby machines" to give birth to more fighting men. The government also enlisted women to serve as military police and drivers.

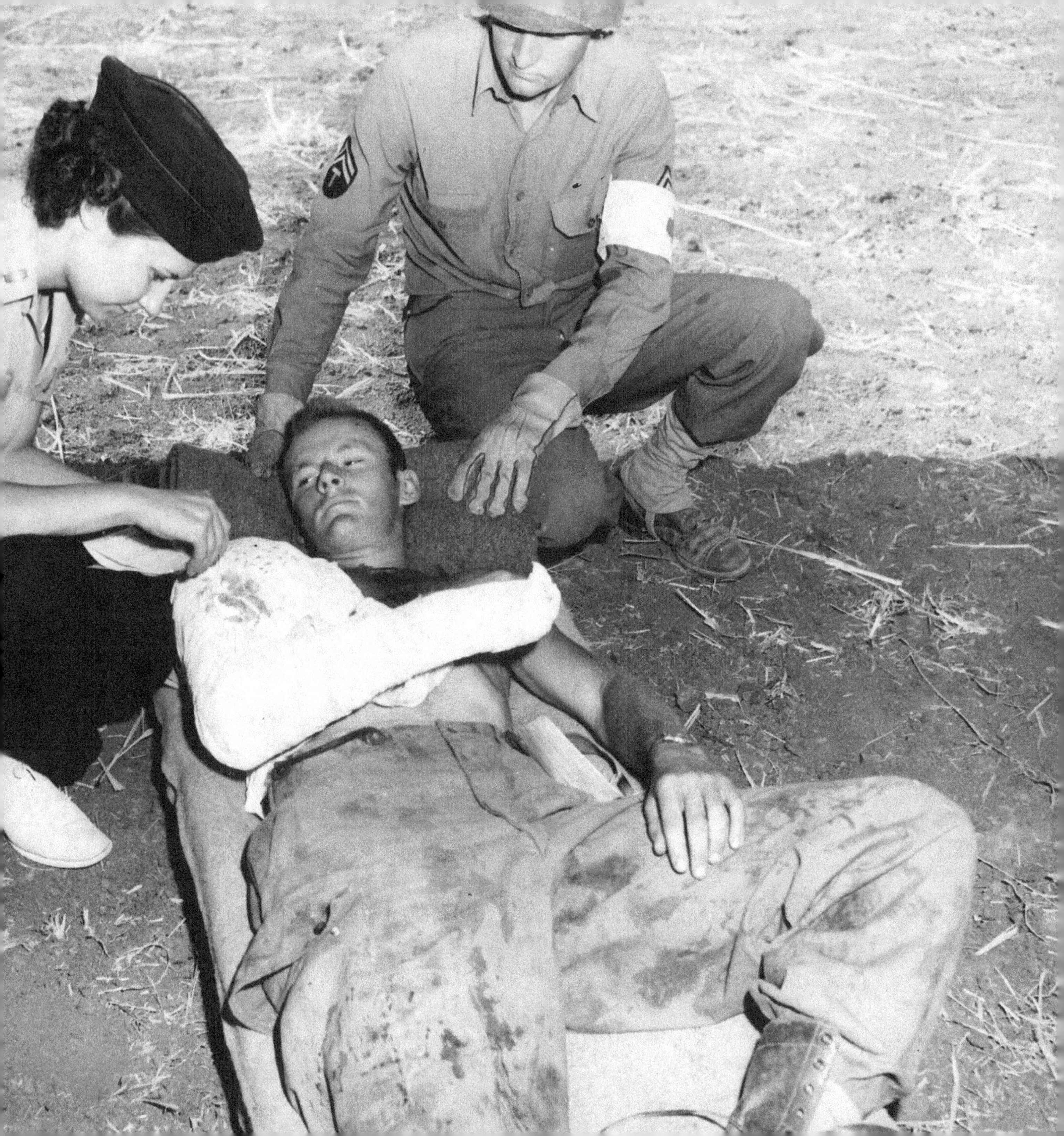

C521366

POLAND

Poland was conquered by Germany and the Soviet Union early in World War II. Women played a major role in the resistance that was active in Poland throughout the rest of the war. They often ran printing presses, carried messages or scouted out enemy positions, but it was mainly Polish men who did the fighting.

In 1944, the people of Warsaw rose up against the Germans who occupied the city. They wanted to liberate Warsaw, and perhaps more of Poland, before the advancing Soviet army could take over the area. They did not want to be controlled by either Germany or the Soviet Union! Women in this struggle carried messages and acted as nurses and medics, but many also took an active part in the fighting. Wanda Gertz was head of the women's sabotage unit, and was highly honored for her bravery and success in disrupting German supply and communications lines.

WARSAW DURING WWII

THE POLISH ARMY

The Germans eventually beat back the uprising, but they recognized the women fighters as members of the Polish Free Army. They set up prisoner-of-war camps to hold over 2000 captured Polish women fighters, in the same way as they held prisoner many thousands of Polish men who had fought.

ROMANIA

One of the major areas where Romanian women contributed during World War II was in the air force. There was a special air transportation unit, The White Squadron, that picked up wounded soldiers and flew them back to hospitals away from the combat area. Most of the unit's pilots were women. The unit operated from 1940 to 1943. Some Romanian women rose to command positions in air units. For instance, the commander of the Bessarabian Squadron, an air transport unit, was Captain Irina Burnaia.

191
123820

PISTOL PACKIN
MAMA

YUGOSLAVIA

Yugoslavia was conquered by Italian and German forces. The Yugoslav National Liberation Movement, under Marshal Tito, fought to push the invaders out of their territory. Of the movement's six million supporters, two million were women. The movement supported a National Liberation Army of over 600,000 soldiers, of whom about 100,000 were women. The army recognized women's rights and women's equality with men. Women often took combat roles, and many died fighting the Italians and Germans. The Liberation Army attracted women to serve by celebrating great women heroes in folk tales and the history of the region.

NO HIDING FROM WAR

In modern history, any war affects not just the countries fighting each other, but their neighbor countries. A major conflict can touch almost every country on Earth. Learn more about what happened during World War II in Baby Professor books like The Allied Powers vs. the Axis Powers in World War II, Did the World War II Spies Have Super-Cool Gadgets?, and The Theaters of World War II: Europe and the Pacific.

INAWA × KOREA 1950
REVOLUTIONARY·WAR·1775-1783 × FRENCH·NAVAL·WAR·1798-1801 × TRIPOLI·1801-1805 × WAR·OF·1812-1815 × FLORIDA·INDIAN·WARS
UNCOMMON VALOR WAS A COMMON VIRTUE
FIDELIS

Visit

BABY PROFESSOR
EDUCATION KIDS

www.BabyProfessorBooks.com

to download Free Baby Professor eBooks
and view our catalog of new and exciting
Children's Books